First Facts®

The Strangest ANIMALS
IN THE WORLD

by Tammy Gagne

CAPSTONE PRESS
a capstone imprint

First Facts are published by Capstone Press,
1710 Roe Crest Drive, North Mankato, Minnesota 56003
www.capstonepub.com

Library of Congress Cataloging-in-Publication Data
Gagne, Tammy, author.
The strangest animals in the world / by Tammy Gagne.
pages cm.—(First facts. All about animals)
Summary: "Interesting facts, colorful photographs, and simple text introduce readers to the
world's strangest animals"—Provided by publisher.
Audience: Ages 6-9.
Audience: K to grade 3.
Includes bibliographical references and index.
ISBN 978-1-4914-2054-6 (library binding)
ISBN 978-1-4914-2240-3 (paperback)
ISBN 978-1-4914-2260-1 (eBook pdf)
1. Animals—Miscellanea—Juvenile literature. I. Title.
QL49.G23 2015
591.02—dc23   2014032098

Editorial Credits
Kathryn Clay, editor; Bobbie Nuytten, designer; Jo Miller, media researcher;
Kathy McColley, production specialist

Photo Credits
Getty Images: Oxford Scientific/Gerard Soury, 13, 22, Photolibrary/Jeff Rotman, 5, 22;
Minden Pictures: David Shale, 15, 22, Wil Meinderts, cover (bottom right) 21, 22; Newscom:
blickwinkle/imago/imago stock & people, 7, 22, CMSP Biology, cover (bottom left), 9, 22,
ZUMA Press/Liu Jian (Xinjiang), 17, 22; Shutterstock: almondd, 10, 22, Andrey Armyagov,
cover (middle), Dudarev Mikhail, cover (top), 1, 11, 22, XIE CHENGXIN, 4, wormig, 22
(map); SuperStock: National Geographic/Tim Laman, 19, 22

Printed in China by Nordica.
0914/CA21401516
092014 008470NORDS15

Table of Contents

Japanese Spider Crab

Tiny bodies. Giant ears. Some animals are certainly strange. From a distance a Japanese spider crab looks like a giant sea spider. Its body is about 15 inches (38 centimeters) wide. But the spider crab's extra-long legs can span 12 feet (3.7 meters).

Fact: Japanese spider crabs live on the ocean floor. Some may live to be 100 years old.

Star-nosed Mole

With its pointy nose, the star-nosed mole definitely looks different. But this odd appearance serves an important purpose. The 22 **tentacles** on the mole's nose can touch 12 objects each second. The tentacles help moles quickly identify if something is **prey** or not. Earthworms and insects that live in or on water make up a large part of their diets.

Fact: Moles live underground and are mostly blind. But they have the best sense of touch of any **mammal** in the world. They can tell if an item is food by touching it less than a second.

tentacle—a long, armlike body part some animals
use to touch, grab, or smell

prey—an animal hunted by another animal for food

mammal—a warm-blooded animal that breathes
air; mammals have hair or fur; female mammals
feed milk to their young

Pink Fairy Armadillo

A pink fairy armadillo might sound like a made-up animal. But it is indeed real. The smallest of all armadillos, it measures just 5 to 6 inches (13 to 15 cm) long. These unusual creatures hide in the sandy soil of Argentina and are rarely seen.

Fact: Most armadillos are completely covered by a brown outer shell. A pink fairy armadillo's pale pink shell only covers the top half of its body.

Fossa

When scientists discovered the fossa, they thought it was a rare cat. While its ears and body do look catlike, its **muzzle** looks more like a dog's. Related to the mongoose, the fossa is the largest **carnivore** on the African island of Madagascar.

muzzle—an animal's nose, mouth, and jaws
carnivore—an animal that eats only meat

Irrawaddy Dolphin

Dolphins are not usually considered strange. But members of this river dolphin **species** look very different from the rest. Unlike other dolphins, Irrawaddy dolphins have no beak. They also do not whistle to one another like other dolphins do. Instead they **communicate** through clicks and buzzing sounds.

Fact: The Irrawaddy dolphin is an **endangered** species. Fewer than 100 of them live in Asia's Mekong River.

species—a group of animals with similar features

communicate—to share information, thoughts, or feelings

endangered—at risk of dying out

Dumbo Octopus

Named after the famous elephant character, the dumbo octopus has giant earlike fins. Similar to the elephant character, dumbo octopuses flap their giant fins to move. These sea creatures are found as far as 3 miles (4.8 km) under the ocean surface. Few people have ever seen one up close.

Fact: Seventeen kinds of dumbo octopuses exist.

Gobi Jerboa

Check out another long-eared animal. The Gobi jerboa's ears are nearly as big as the rodent's body. A skilled jumper, this animal also has very long legs. Combine these features, and you have one of the oddest-looking animals in the world.

Fact: Gobi jerboas can survive a wide temperature range. In the summer the Gobi Desert can reach 104 degrees Fahrenheit (40 degrees Celsius). Winter temperatures can fall to -40 degrees Fahrenheit (-40 degrees Celsius).

Superb Bird of Paradise

In many animal species males are often more colorful than females. But the superb bird of paradise takes this quality to an extreme. The male can raise his feathers into a striking blue and black cape. He then performs a special hopping dance to get the attention of a female.

Fact: Female members of this species have black-brown feathers. The colors blend in with the surroundings to hide the birds from predators.

Sea Lamprey

A sea lamprey's jawless mouth makes it look like a creature from a scary movie. Its round mouth holds rows and rows of teeth. Sea lampreys attach themselves to other fish and suck out their blood. Only one in seven fish that a sea lamprey attacks is likely to survive.

Fact: Sea lampreys once lived only in the ocean. Today thousands have made their way into the Great Lakes of North America.

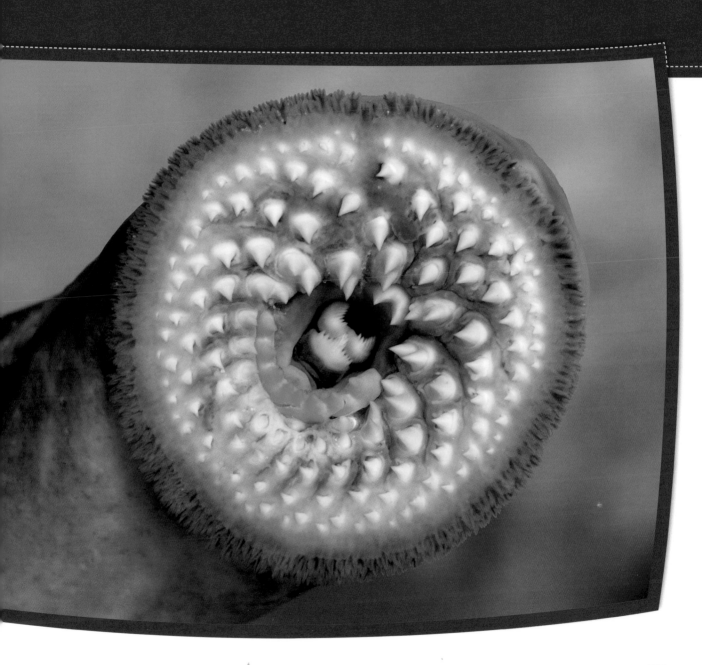

Range Map

Japanese Spider Crab		Irrawaddy Dolphin	
Star-nosed Mole		Superb Bird of Paradise	
Pink Fairy Armadillo		Gobi Jerboa	
Fossa		Dumbo Octopus	
		Sea Lamprey	

Glossary

carnivore (KAHR-nuh-vohr)—an animal that eats only meat

communicate (kuh-MYOO-nuh-kate)—to share information, thoughts, or feelings

endangered (in-DAYN-juhrd)—at risk of dying out

mammal (MAM-uhl)—a warm–blooded animal that breathes air; mammals have hair or fur; female mammals feed milk to their young

muzzle (MUHZ-uhl)—an animal's nose, mouth, and jaws

predator (PRED-uh-tur)—an animal that hunts other animals for food

prey (PRAY)—an animal hunted by another animal for food

species (SPEE-sheez)—a group of animals with similar features

tentacle (TEN-tuh-kuhl)—a long, armlike body part some animals use to touch, grab, or smell

Critical Thinking Using the Common Core

1. Describe how male and female birds of paradise are different. Next, explain why they are different. (Key Ideas and Details)

2. Look at the fact box on page 20. What may have caused sea lampreys to move into the Great Lakes? (Integration of Knowledge and Ideas)

23

Read More

Berger, Melvin, and Gilda Berger. *101 Freaky Animals*. New York: Scholastic, 2010.

Hearst, Michael. *Unusual Creatures: A Mostly Accurate Account of Some of Earth's Strangest Animals*. San Francisco: Chronicle Books, 2012.

Marsh, Laura. *National Geographic Readers: Weird Sea Creatures*. Washington, D.C.: National Geographic Children's Books, 2012.

Internet Sites

FactHound offers a safe, fun way to find Internet sites related to this book. All of the sites on FactHound have been researched by our staff.

Here's all you do:
Visit www.facthound.com
Type in this code: 9781491420546

Super-cool stuff! Check out projects, games and lots more at **www.capstonekids.com**

Index